The *Alan Ward*
Railway
Sketchbook

A compilation of scribbles, working sketches, & completed paintings
from the Alan Ward Collection

The Alan Ward Railway Sketchbook

A compilation of scribbles, working sketches, & completed paintings from the Alan Ward Collection

ISBN 978-1-900340-23-6

Designed by The Alan Ward Collection

Published by Mainline & Maritime Ltd
3 Broadleaze, Upper Seagry, Nr Chippenham SN15 5EY
www.mainlineandmaritime.co.uk

Printed in the United Kingdom by Contract Publishing UK (CPUK) Ltd
www.contractpublishinguk.co.uk

Foreword

*Alan lets us in on his world by letting us see the
process he goes through to make his paintings.
I have been fascinated by art since I was a young lad,
but worked out a long time ago that I had no talent for it.*

*This book shows the talent needed from the subject
and its composition to the final painting.
Railways and Wildlife have been part of my
life for as long as I can remember.
I hope you enjoy this book as much as I did.*

Dr Pete Waterman OBE DL

Introduction

A valued patron of mine visiting a recent show wondered why a book of my railway and transport paintings had not been published. I explained that a few years ago one had been planned and prepared for a publisher, only to be shelved at the eleventh hour.

In the middle of my 'annual' studio tidy-up, rummaging through plan chests and files full of sketches, I was amazed at the volume that had accrued over the years. Soon the studio floor was covered with material. Some of the emerging sketches and scribbles I had considered lost, whilst others I could not even remember doing.

Now is the time to convert all this newly discovered material into a book. As most of the work was pencil and charcoal, it was decided to publish in monochrome. Much of the ensuing material and examples of completed paintings have creatively benefitted from black and white reproduction. We hope that you agree.

Alan Ward

The drawings & sketches

*The artist's armoury of materials and equipment is vast.
When working in the field, I always carry a small rucksack packed
with everything I might need. Subjects are not going to keep still
whilst you search for the right pencil, putty rubber or pen. Most of
the time you have literally minutes to complete a sketch before the
subject steams, flies or sails away. Even sketching people
can be a challenge. Can you sit still for an hour or so?*

*Sometimes lightning thumbnails can act as an 'aide memoir'
to an idea when you are back in the studio. This, accompanied
by a few scribbled notes, is often enough to jog the memory
and set the creative wheels in motion. Many of the
completed works in the collection have started
out in this way.*

LAWRENCE HILL

This sketch resulted in a completed painting. Looking at the scribbled notation on the picture, it would seem that I was more preoccupied with getting the colour of the signals right. It would also appear that I could not decide which loco to include. The one on the bridge carrying a Midland branch line seems to be a cross between a class 7F and 4F. It did end up in the final painting as a 4F. The Great Western motive power is much more obvious as a Castle Class 4-6-0 heading a maroon coach set bound for Temple Meads.

OVER AND UNDER AT LAWRENCE HILL

Black Prince at Bishop's Lydeard

I visited a West Somerset Railway Spring Gala a few years ago with the sole purpose of sketching the restored BR 9F 2-10-0 Black Prince in a suitable location for a water colour painting commissioned by a collector. Although not a shed in the strict sense of the word, the location at Bishops Lydeard took my eye. Particularly for the fact that I could introduce a little drama to the painting by adding a scheduled down working to Minehead headed by the Somerset & Dorset incumbent class 7F. This, I thought, would produce an atmospheric shed style scene whilst capturing the feverish activity which always accompanies these popular heritage railway events.

Sketch for water colour painting of Black Prince on Bishops Lydeard. Possibly a 7F on the 'down' 88. View looking towards Taunton.

9F 2-10-0 BLACK PRINCE

Evercreech Junction

The Somerset & Dorset.
You cannot help but be inspired by such
an iconic railway. A railway that has
passed into folk legend and yet
still captures the imaginations of
young and old alike. Those
that were lucky enough to
travel on the 'slow & dirty'
on such sheduled services
as the Pines Express are
always willing to relish
and share those moments.

This 6B charcoal
pencil drawing was
fast-tracked, going
straight into the finished work
inspired by various pieces of archive reference
material plus a little imagination
and, indeed, artist's licence.

Royal Scot departs Bath with the 'up' Pines Express

In the heyday of the Somerset and Dorset, a busy schedule of workings from the Midlands and North of England arrived on Bath shed which gave local trainspotters a real treat. Word soon got around that 46100 'Royal Scot' had arrived. And much to their delight, stayed around for a short while, conducting various duties. Because of the local interest, I produced this finished charcoal pencil drawing of the occasion which was subsequently published and added to the collection. An interesting little footnote to this scene is the ubiquitous S&D 4-4-0 Class 2P working up from the Somerset & Dorset shed.

"Royal Scot" leaves Bath with the up Pines Express

The Mess Room

The following sketches formed the basis of an idea for a painting inspired by the colourful railwaymen I met and chatted to at railway shows throughout the South West.

They willingly shared memories, experiences and anecdotes of the steam era. Some were happy to sit for the quick sketches that would form the basis of the picture. I am often asked where the shed was based. It is in fact a figment of my imagination. The scene is depicted towards the end of steam and reflects an eclectic mix of motive power consistent with late days of British Rail. What came to light was the hierarchy and pecking order commonly found in mess rooms throughout the regions. The old stagers commanded a great deal of respect in those days.

The atmosphere was always thick with cigarette and tobacco smoke as well as steam from the constantly boiling cast iron kettle on the stove.

Couldn't make my mind up about the siting of the shed for the mess room painting when these sketches were dreamt up. There does seem to be a heavy Great Western influence however. It was in the pursuit of anonymity that I eventually drew a BR Standard class 5, a Southern Mogul and possibly a GWR Hall. I think however, on reflection, that I was more preoccupied with character studies of the railway men; their status, what they did, where they sat, what they smoked, what they ate, what they read and what form they studied.

THE MESS ROOM

Railway people and personalities

I do my fair share of standard three-quarter angle portraits and paintings of locomotives during the course of a working year. This is often what is commissioned. But wherever possible, I will always include figures in a scene. They give a drawing or painting scale and depth, and introduce an element of social and industrial history.

Happily, it is still possible to sketch and paint railwaymen and women in the working environment. A commitment to historical accuracy by the heritage railway movement has made this possible. You might think that some of the sketches included in this book were produced at the zenith of steam. However, many are from the present day. It might be interesting to work out which ones are which!

Railways do seem to attract their fair share of characters. Let's face it, where would they be without them? Some of the tasks and duties undertaken in the day to day running of these railways are high profile. Engine drivers, firemen, signalmen, station masters etc., but the day to day running of the railway depends equally on less glamorous but equally important roles. Ticket collectors to tea ladies, cleaners to conductors, no modern heritage railway could function effectively without them. Pride in appearance comes top of the list whatever the task. Freshly pressed uniforms, shiny buttons, polished boots and a freshly cut buttonhole from the station garden for the guard's lapel.

Tickets please!!!
How often has that familiar request rung out over the decades? I could not resist producing a sketch of this familiar stalwart of the railway scene working as a volunteer on one of our heritage railways. We have all heard stories relating to passengers locking themselves in the carriage toilet to avoid the ticket collector whilst travelling free. Of course, that was way back in the halcyon days of British Rail. We wouldn't dream of committing such a larceny today would we?

A lady on the platform wearing a Santa hat and enjoying a nice staff 'cuppa' from the station buffet. It must be time for the Santa Specials! It's a bit chilly sketching outdoors at this time of year (you can see the steam rising from the plastic cup), but I could not resist this drawing, although I have to admit that it was completed as a charcoal sketch back in the warmth of my studio.

'Portrait of a seasonal helper' might be a good caption for the picture at what is a vital time for heritage railways to secure much needed revenue for the coming year.

On the footplate and maintenance

*Two studies of present day locations.
The first is a duty driver on the West Somerset Railway. I sketched him as he chatted to Spring Gala visitors after having steamed one of the 4-6-0 Manors to Minehead from Bishops Lydeard. Plenty of stories and anecdotes were on the menu for the assembled crowds.*

The second sketch I think, captures the unseen and often unsung routine work of maintaining and restoring diesel locomotives at the Williton depot of the West Somerset. Dirty, greasy and often uncomfortable activities. From the expression on the fitter's face you can tell that they just love it!

WILLITON BASED WESTERN CAMPAIGNER

Engine drivers

The character comes with the job. And I don't know about you but I certainly wanted to be an engine driver in my trainspotting days. These two sketches of past and present day men of steam are versions of that cult status that inspired us all. It hasn't diminished over the years either. The expressions of wonderment and awe on youngsters' faces at the sight of steam locomotives are a joy to behold.

This archive charcoal sketch of a British Rail engine driver oiling the bearings on a mainline express loco on-shed probably in the late fifties, early sixties vividly portrays the pride and sense of purpose footplate men had in their work. This was, as I recall, a reference sketch for a shed painting featuring locomotives in various stages of readiness for the day's duties. Needless to say, the picture was never produced but the drawing survived in all its sepia tone 2B charcoal pencil glory. Perhaps having been re-discovered, it could be used as a reference for my next painting commission.

Dunster Gardeners

Pretty much all of the heritage railways in the country rely on armies of unpaid, unswerving volunteers in order to operate and maintain services. They are the grass roots of a movement, without whom, steam would not survive.

On a visit to Dunster Station a few years ago to do some sketching, I happened on a delightful couple who were lovingly tending the station gardens. They were very well versed, not only about railways, but gardening in general. After confounding and confusing me with exotic names of herbaceous border plants, I managed to turn the conversation around to artistic matters.

They were more than pleased to learn that I might do some drawings of them, one of which I have included in the book in the knowledge that this vital part of the railway's infrastructure has not gone unnoticed.

Charitable donations

Whilst on Dunster station that particular day, I was approached by a very smart, and indeed, dapper gentleman who seemed to have an air of authority and had taken more than a passing interest in my exchanges with the volunteer gardeners. He turned out to be the station master and a well-known pillar of the community.

I felt another sketch coming on. The suggestion was made, but it would cost me! I was very politely informed that it would be appropriate to make a small donation to the station fund. "How small?" I asked. This retort was taken in the spirit it was intended and greeted with a big grin. I left that day slightly lighter in pocket but much richer in artistic terms. The resultant drawing was finished, and filed to gather dust in the studio over the years. On re-discovery, I felt it deserved to be included on historic and artistic merit alone.

Preoccupations with paddle steamers

We all know of the country's historic maritime railway connections, so I thought it relevant in a book on railways to include a section on one of my favourite paddle steamers: the Waverley. From the first moment I saw her majestically steaming up the River Avon and into the port of Bristol, I was hooked and became a lifelong fan.

Her movements and activities over the years have inspired many sketches and resultant paintings. One of my fondest memories was being commissioned by the Waverley Steam Navigation Co to produce a painting and subsequently being invited on board to sign copies of the resultant fine-art prints during a cruise down the Bristol Channel. Apart from generating funds for the ongoing restoration project, my lasting memory of that day was steaming back up the River Avon into Bristol under the Clifton Suspension Bridge on a glorious summer's day.

Waverley returns to Bristol

The original sketches for this picture appear to be lost or maybe in the hands of a private collector. Either way the end result featured on this page was, I feel, worth it. What I did find during the ransacking of my studio were a few marine scribbles and doodles which must have played some part in the production of the original work.

Ideas for paintings manifest themselves from the artist's sketchbook, and looking at some of these examples reminds me of other marine pictures I painted but, for the life of me, I can't remember where they are or where they went. Talk about being all at sea!

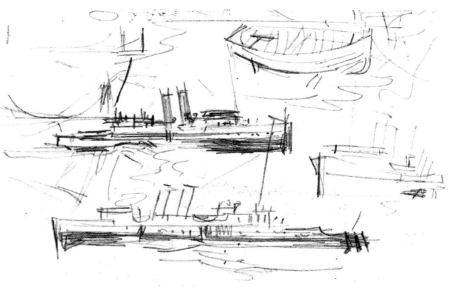

Tornado

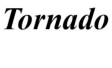

After the massive build-up of interest in the construction and completion of the first steam locomotive to be built in Britain for fifty years, 60163 Peppercorn class A1 pacific 'Tornado' was immediately taken to the heart of the nation. Its subsequent introduction to main line running drew massive crowds and created star status wherever it steamed. It continues to do so.

Images of it were legion. So much so, I felt it worthwhile adding my own and produced an impressionist painting plus drawings and scribble ideas. I think Ribblehead Viaduct was in my mind as the backdrop to a major painting. But that's as far as it got. Finding these sketches though might just rekindle my original interest in what is a most worthy subject.

European connections

Everyone likes a challenge don't they?
Well, I really wasn't quite sure what I had taken on
with this painting. I did several exhibitions
at the Upton-upon-Severn Jazz Festival over the years,
exhibiting some of my Jazz portraits as well
as a mix of Railways, Wildlife and West Country work.
It was during one of these exhibitions that a
member of a German band playing at the festival

came into the exhibition and spent some time
viewing the paintings. After intently viewing
one particular work, the musician approached me
and enquired if I would be interested in accepting
a commission. The work he was studying was
entitled 'End of Shift'.

It is a character study of an engine driver and
fireman leaving the shed after a hard day's toil on the
footplate. It was a very atmospheric picture of a simmering
railway yard at sunset somewhere in the
shires. This was the type of painting he wished to
commission but, there was a proviso. The scene had
to be in East Germany before unification at what is
now a world heritage site: The Coal Mines of
Zollverein in the late fifties. Added to which would be
German locos of the time, plus the whole seven
members of the band. Ouch! I did say it was a
challenge! And after a little haggle over fees,
I eventually accepted the commission.

Now I had to meet all of the band for sketches plus
photographs as the commission involved virtually
seven portraits. After a good deal of research, a final
sketch was prepared, copied and mailed to Vienna
where it met with much approval. There now just
remained the simple matter of painting this huge
canvas. Needless to say, it took quite a time and
now hangs in a prominent place in Vienna.

END OF GIG
The Bourbon Street Stompers

The Gresley Birds Series

There is something a touch romantic and quintessentially English about naming the class of LNER A4 Pacific railway locomotives after our rich diversity of wildlife. This holds very true for me particularly in the light of my passionate artistic involvement with both. It also provided me with a flash of inspiration! Why not combine the two elements into a series of evocative railway paintings.

'Seagull' on the Forth Bridge was one of the first to come to mind and alas, was one of the sketches that was never produced as a painting. In the following pages however, you will see that many of the other ensuing sketches were followed through. And whilst the production line has come to a halt, there are still many subjects still to do.

And I'm sure the famous CME of the LNER would have approved.

The initial series of 'The Gresley Birds' paintings and wildlife prints amounts to five, namely:
1. Kingfisher Country. 2. Golden Eagle in the Glens.
3. Mallard in flight. 4. Wild Swan in Winter.
5. Quicksilver Fox.

Many of my sketchbooks are filled with birds of prey. I find them majestic and indeed awesome in predatory flight. The Peregrine falcon for instance was the subject of a re-introduction programme to the Avon Gorge well within sight of Brunel's Suspension Bridge. Many sketches came from that scene particularly because it was so easy to view them from the Bristol Downs. They must have been around when the GWR ran along the Gorge from Bristol to Portishead. Some picture that would have made.

What's left? Well, look at the list:
60018 Sparrow Hawk, 60019 Bittern, 60020 Guillemot, 60025 Falcon, 60026 Kestrel, 60027 Merlin, 60028 Sea Eagle, 60029 Woodcock, 60030 Great Snipe, 60031 Golden Plover, 60032 Gannet, 60033 Seagull, 60034 Peregrine and 4469 Gadwall.

That makes another fourteen possible subjects to add to the series. Hmm,... Food for thought.

Kingfisher Country

A bird that features greatly in my wildlife collection is the fabulous Kingfisher. I have sat at tiny isolated pools on the rivers and streams of North Devon whilst trout fishing and waited hours for a fleeting glimpse and a flash of turquoise.

I always carry a sketchbook on my travels piscatorial and otherwise, so whilst the image is fresh in my mind, I can set it down in rapid scribble form to be reviewed in the studio and converted into a completed work at a later date. It automatically followed that this fascination would find a niche in the selection of LNER A4 Pacific No. 4483 Kingfisher as one of the paintings to be included in the collection.

KINGFISHER COUNTRY

Golden Eagle in the Glens

From eerie aloft does the Eagle descend. What better background scene for a painting of Gresley's A4 Pacific No.4482 Golden Eagle than the rugged, breathtaking highlands of Scotland? I know that I made up several sketches for this picture, but this is the only one that seems to have survived. It shows both birds at the nest but I recall that the scene looked a bit too busy, so I decided to leave the male out. The basic angle remained roughly the same for the finished work. Several of Gresley's A4s were named after birds of prey, possibly by virtue of the locomotive's sleek and swift lines.

GOLDEN EAGLE IN THE GLENS

Mallard in flight

In the light of recent anniversaries and events I feel that I could write volumes about A4 Pacific No.4468 Mallard, one of the world's most famous locomotives and holder of the world steam traction record of 126mph. But, bearing in mind this book's artistic aim and purpose, I will restrict my historic homage to a few lines. I'm sure others will do it far more justice. As a painting however, it takes its rightful place in the Gresley Birds Series and Collection.

The picture portrays Mallard's historic record breaking run, scattering flights of duck off the water and skywards in the process. The sketch for this picture almost suggested itself and virtually became the completed work. The only difference being a technical correction with the addition of the wheel valance to the streamlining for the sake of historical accuracy.

MALLARD IN FLIGHT

Quicksilver Fox

The title of this picture was a combination of the names of two of the A4 Pacifics: 'Quicksilver' and 'Silver Fox'. I think I was attempting to make a comparison between the speed, power and wily agility of the fox in the wild to the perfomance of the locomotives.

Here again, I produced several pencil sketch ideas for the painting, but only managed to find one. It wasn't the scene I ended up producing but, I think, still gives a good insight into the way a picture develops creatively and progresses to the final stages.

QUICKSILVER FOX

Wild Swan in Winter

There seems to be little logic in the selection of a subject to add to a series. This picture materialised as the result of some sketches for Christmas cards. The cards turned out quite well, so I thought it might be a good idea to add the final picture to the 'Gresley Birds Series'. A4 pacific No.4467 'Wild Swan' seemed to lend itself to the atmospheric wintery scene.

Pages of an old sketch book I found were covered in scruffy, thumbnail scribbles of swans in various states of flight and landing postures. However, this is the only one I felt was worthy of reproduction. All the possible angles for this picture were covered in the sketches.

WILD SWAN IN WINTER

HST north of Teignmouth

Commissioned works play an extremely important role in my everyday working life. The sketch reproduced here saw the start of one of these works. The brief was to create a painting that captured the colours of the moment, both in terms of livery and location. The impressive sandstone cliffs of South Devon were chosen as the backdrop to an HST picking up speed on the curve out of Teignmouth station.

The diesel was to sport the precise First Great Western livery of the humorously nicknamed 'fag packet' design. The colours of which referred to the Rothmans cigarette packaging of the time. There are not too many diesel paintings in the collection at the moment, so I was quite pleased to accept this commission and add the finished painting to the catalogue. It is my intention to produce many more sketches and paintings of the diesel scene over the coming years.

HST NORTH OF TEIGNMOUTH

Bristol Blue Pullman

The epitome of style and élan, a shimmering blue streak cutting through the countryside on a crystal clear day. Well, perhaps that's just a bit too much poetic licence!

The introduction of the Blue Pullman service to the Western Region in the late fifties however, did bring a degree of hitherto unknown style and up-market luxury with the starched white coats of the on-board stewards attending to the whims and wishes of the commuting business classes. It certainly cut the mustard with a certain young lad encamped on Chipping Sodbury Station, Ian Allan loco book firmly clenched in hand. The initial preparatory sketch of this scene for the painting was commissioned by that very same boy who, in later life, wanted the evocative scene recaptured for posterity.

There is nothing much left of the scene nowadays, so a lot of guesswork was needed in its recreation.

BRISTOL BLUE PULLMAN

The Industrial Scene

I decided to devote a section of the book to the industrial scene, based on a few more dedicated sketches coming to light. Many of the completed works were in charcoal. I think the intense blacks and greys of the medium suit the subject well. In a way it brings out the character and depth of these little leviathans. One of the thumbnail scribbles illustrated formed the basis of a painting of the narrow gauge Welsh slate quarries. The locomotive pictured is a completed charcoal sketch of a Barclay standard 0-4-0 industrial locomotive. A number of these little pocket size workhorses were built in the late twenties and early thirties to serve the Steel Company of Wales.

Here's a finished charcoal drawing of 0-4-0 'Joan'
and another sketch of a loco straight out of the Avonside
Engineering Company, Bristol, stable. Bristol was also
the home of another famous engineering company:
Peckett & Sons Ltd., of the Atlas Engineering Works, St Georges.

These industrial 0-6-0s are restored and fully operational.
'Portbury' below is running to this day on the Bristol
Harbour Railway, delighting children and enthusiasts alike.

Industrial Garratts

Until I was commissioned to paint an industrial scene incorporating one of these little powerful 0-4-4-0 Beyer Peacock Garratts, I knew very little about them. Apparently they could do the work of two conventional industrial locos but were quite rare and sparsley distributed around the British industrial scene. I found them quite charming in an artistic sort of way, and did several sketches from reference to give me an idea for the final composition. It had to be set in a heavily industrial landscape probably somewhere in South Wales where I believe one or two of these locos were operating at the time.

BEYER-PEACOCK GARRATT 0-4-4-0 AT WORK

Lost & Found Sketches

A pannier tank puffs through Ashton Gate station against a backdrop of the Clifton Suspension Bridge with a Bristol-bound freight train in the late fifties. This little doodle was used as the basis for a small impressionist acrylic painting. There is much interest in the Portishead line at the moment where it is planned to reopen it to passenger services in the near future. The view of a Great Western prairie tank steaming again through the Avon Gorge and under the suspension bridge would be a magnificent sight to behold.

The sketch below was the result of a request for an idea to commemorate St. George's Day. The little boy waving the flag, the locomotive; St George. That's as far as it got!

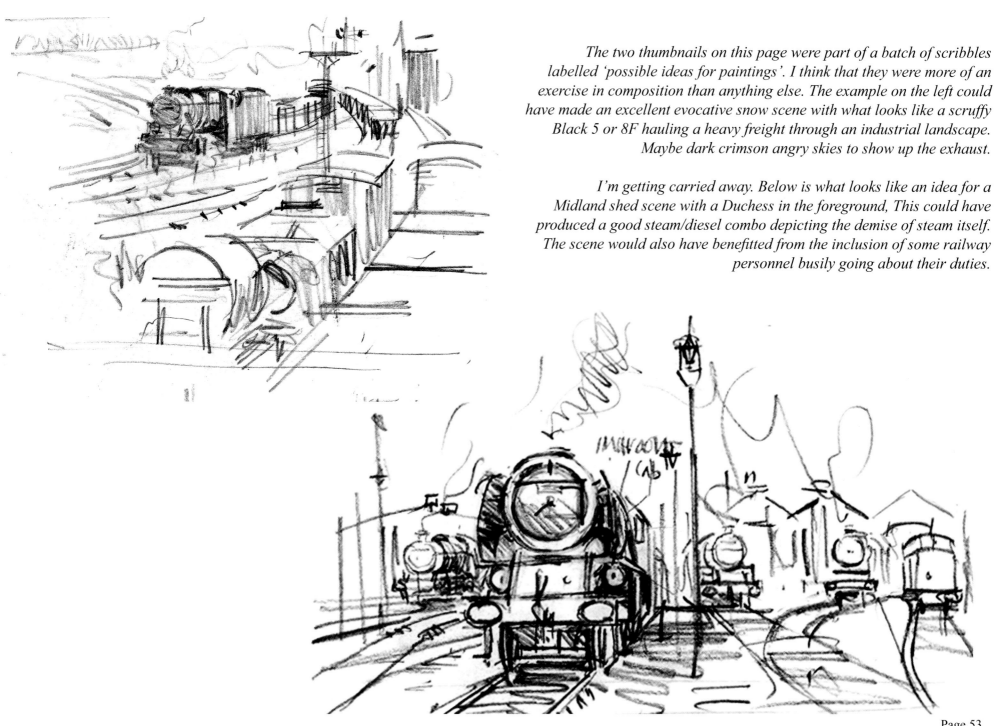

The two thumbnails on this page were part of a batch of scribbles labelled 'possible ideas for paintings'. I think that they were more of an exercise in composition than anything else. The example on the left could have made an excellent evocative snow scene with what looks like a scruffy Black 5 or 8F hauling a heavy freight through an industrial landscape. Maybe dark crimson angry skies to show up the exhaust.

I'm getting carried away. Below is what looks like an idea for a Midland shed scene with a Duchess in the foreground, This could have produced a good steam/diesel combo depicting the demise of steam itself. The scene would also have benefitted from the inclusion of some railway personnel busily going about their duties.

Shed Scenes

Ashes, coal dust, smoke, steam oil, railwaymen, grease and gravitas. Railway shed sketches and paintings just knock me for six. I love producing them, even though they take twice as long as conventional pictures to paint simply because there are more locos in them. But it is well worth the extra effort, even if you do have to get into the studio at the crack of dawn to complete them! They also offer real opportunities to experiment with styles.

I am a great fan of the French Impressionists, in particular Monet & Sisley. Monet's paintings of Gare Saint Lazare and the railway bridge at Argenteuil are classic examples of how to portray an atmospheric railway scene without the encumbrance of unnecessary detail. Many of the best paintings however, do include copious detail, but are still very much dependent on composition and light. I have included an impressionist rendering of a shed scene with a vaguely familiar 8F in the foreground. There is little detail, simply broad accidental brush strokes which sometimes come off and sometimes don't. I leave you to judge which is best.

EVENING ACTION AT BARROW ROAD

SUNNY MORNING ON THE S&D SHED - CLASS 2Ps AT BATH

AFTERNOON SUNSHINE AT BARROW ROAD ROUNDHOUSE

NIGHTSHIFT DUTIES AT BARROW ROAD

IMPRESSION OF AN 8F

Isambard Kingdom Brunel

The engineering feats of Isambard Kingdom Brunel feature in many of my sketches and paintings, from scenes of the magnificent broad gauge 'Rover' class 8 foot singles to the iconic Clifton Suspension Bridge. A wealth of subject matter available at the artist's fingertips. Maritime wonders such as the S.S. Great Britain; architectural masterpieces such as the passenger shed at Temple Meads, all preserved for posterity.

Rediscovered reference sketches of this rich industrial age will undoubtedly form the basis of many new works to come.

This sketch idea of what the passenger shed at Temple Meads might have looked like in the late 1880s through the hustle and bustle of broad gauge services could be the basis of a future project. Perhaps with the introduction of a Hawthorn class 2-4-0 (left) into a centre road of the station. The sketch also suggests that there was feverish Post Office activity and presence. With some time spent researching period costume and rolling stock etc., it could turn into a major work.

Temple Meads 1890s

The 'Rover' class 8 foot broad gauge single wheelers were the Great Western Railway's premier locomotives of the day, hauling express services such as the 'Flying Dutchman' and 'Cornishman'. Locomotive names included such evocative titles as Dragon, Eupatoria, Great Western, Emperor, Warlock and Amazon. Sadly, the last broad gauge Cornishman service departed Paddington on May 20th 1892 and into the history books. Standard gauge had arrived. This sketch of a 'Rover' class is based on a regular Bristol visitor namely; 'Iron Duke'.

The down Cornishman passing Uphill Junction is the other sketch which shows a standard gauge goods train waiting on the down line from Weston-super-Mare.

BROAD GAUGE DAYS - KEYNSHAM STATION

BOX TUNNEL IN WINTER

PENRICE CASTLE AT BOX TUNNEL

'THE BRISTOLIAN' AT BOX TUNNEL

CASTLE CLASS 4-6-0 'ISAMBARD KINGDOM BRUNEL' AT BATH

'CITY OF TRURO' AT SYDNEY GARDENS

Drawing on more ideas

The ability to produce lightning sketches and paintings is one of the pre-requisites of a well-known and much admired artistic brotherhood in Bristol. Its famous 'two hour' sketches produced without reference and no prior knowledge of the subject matter are universally acclaimed.

As a past member of that society, I can recall the degree of panic that would set in when the chairman of the regular weekly meetings chalked on the blackboard the subject for the evening. Some of the subjects were so obscure the studio was often a sea of blank expressions. Creativity however, always prevailed and much great and inspired work was produced. My sketch here is the result of one such session.

The subject? Auld Lang Syne! The completed two-hour impressionist painting was of an A4 hauling the 'Flying Scotsman'. Appropriate or what!

Miscellaneous sketch. Barrow Road looking towards the coaling stage, sheds, gasholders and Bristol beyond. The loco is a British Railways Standard Class 5 heading a Gloucester bound local. This could produce a compelling atmospheric painting with the introduction of possibly two or three more locos in the background around the stages. Dating is late fifties, early sixties.

Another miscellaneous sketch. Looks like the coaling stage again at Barrow Road, Bristol. An 0-6-0 4F shunting empty coach stock in the foreground. The interesting part of this composition is the walled garden backing on to the railway. Looks like Mum hanging out the washing with her little boy assisting. How the clothes ever stayed clean though is a mystery. A nice touch is the suggestion of a small kitchen garden. Maybe some runner beans and a few cabbages. Including this little piece of social history would make for a compelling picture.

GWR Country Station

Branch line railways have assumed folk status with many enthusiasts and casual observers alike. This particular sketch depicts one of the stations on the 'Strawberry Line' which ran from the mainline station at Yatton, through Cheddar to Wells and on to Witham. This was the fastest way at the time to get Cheddar strawberries to markets in Bristol and beyond.

The railway and station buildings finally ended up as a stone yard and housing complex. The main Sandford and Banwell station building however, was fully restored, so it was possible to sketch it in full detail and select one of the little GWR prairie tank locos that ran regularly on the line to include in a full painting.

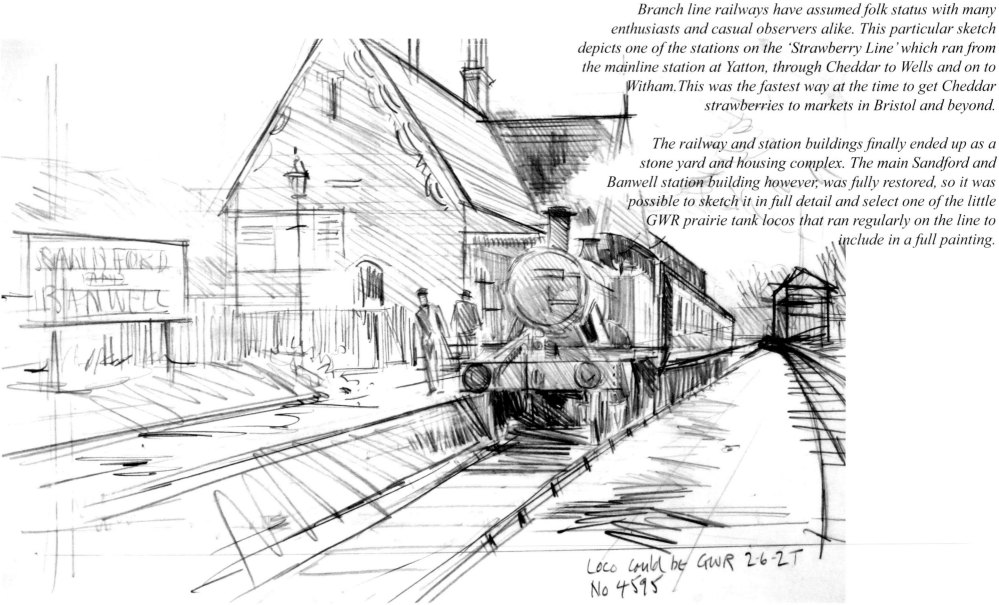

Loco could be GWR 2-6-2T No 4595

GWR COUNTRY STATION

THE STRAWBERRY SPECIAL

LAST TRAIN TO CHEDDAR

The Great Gathering

Sunday 7 July 2013 was a notable date, certainly in my diary. Pencilled in was a coach trip to the National Railway Museum at York. The six remaining Gresley A4 Pacifics had been assembled in the great hall for the very last time. It was a 'once in a lifetime' opportunity to view and artistically record this magnificent spectacle before they were scattered across the globe. I took some reference pictures and scribbled a few notes on angles to take back to the studio.

I had decided to produce a painting of this historic event, but wanted to create my own working, classic line-up, composition. I have included some of the annotated scribbles and the final working sketches for the painting. The medium I chose was oil on canvas measuring some four and a half feet. It needed to be large to accommodate the detail. The work took roughly three months to complete and was duly published as a limited edition fine-art print.

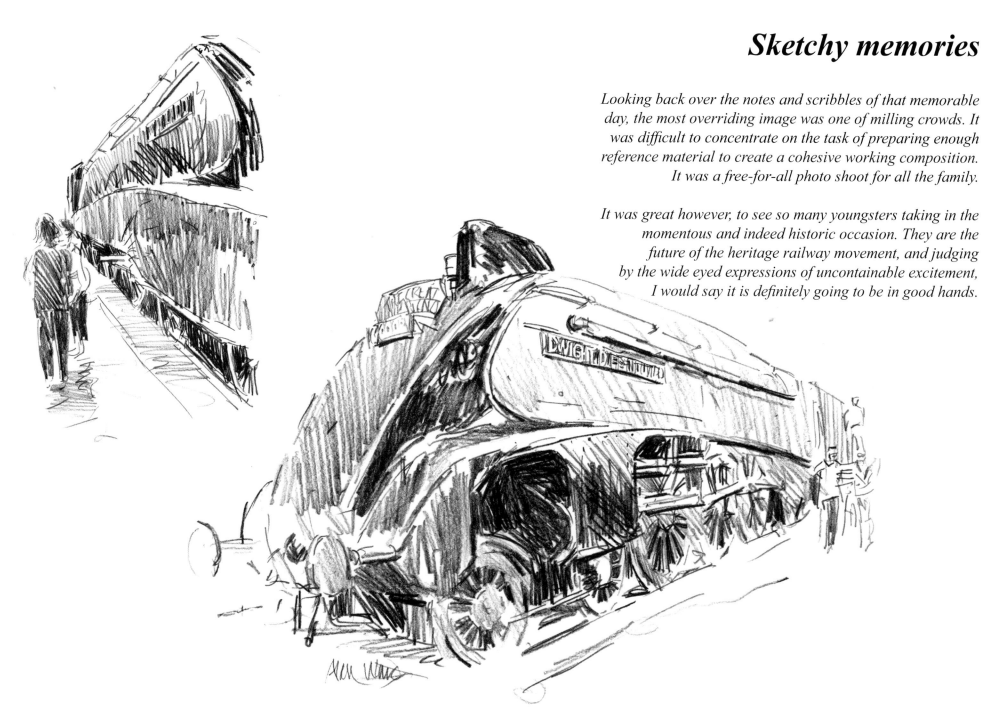

Sketchy memories

Looking back over the notes and scribbles of that memorable day, the most overriding image was one of milling crowds. It was difficult to concentrate on the task of preparing enough reference material to create a cohesive working composition. It was a free-for-all photo shoot for all the family.

It was great however, to see so many youngsters taking in the momentous and indeed historic occasion. They are the future of the heritage railway movement, and judging by the wide eyed expressions of uncontainable excitement, I would say it is definitely going to be in good hands.

*The working drawing and final composition
for the Great Gathering oil painting pictured is the one
committed to canvas (right). This is the stage when
the underpainting begins to take shape.
Laying colour washes and glazes combine to give
an idea of the way the contrast and light of the painting
will take shape. The final stages of the painting involve the
application of opaque body colour and finite detail.*

LNER 4-6-2 Class A4s Left to right: No.60007 Sir Nigel Gresley / No.60008 Dwight D Eisenhower /
No.60009 Union of South Africa / No.4464 Bittern / No.4468 Mallard / No.4489 Dominion of Canada

THE GREAT GATHERING

Unrebuilt Southern Pacifics

Back in our trainspotting days when Bulleid Pacifics were affectionately known as 'spam cans', their penchant for wheel slip and distinctive 'bark' made them a favourite with encamped platform ragamuffins throughout the South and West of England. Some were allocated to the Somerset & Dorset in the fifties and worked mainly double-headed to tackle the steep gradients of the Mendip Hills in Somerset.

They have featured in many of my paintings over the years. I find them a huge challenge artistically because of the vast, flat areas of cladding. There are no subtle boiler curves, handrails or steam pipes to create three dimensions and depth. Simply a huge mirror on which to paint a reflected landscape over the rippled panels. Often it is the simplest rendering that creates the most effect.

Perhaps it is fitting that I chose to mark the sad occasion of the closure of the S&D with a painting of the two Bulleid Pacifics 'Bude' & 'Biggin Hill' heading the last southbound enthusiasts' special on S&D metals over Midford Viaduct. The final painting I chose to title, I think appropriately: 'REQUIEM FOR THE SOMERSET & DORSET'

REQUIEM FOR THE SOMERSET & DORSET

The Golden Arrow

The down Golden Arrow boat train service from Victoria to Dover in the early fifties. Can there be a more evocative railway setting than this iconic train steaming past Battersea Power Station and Factory Junction hauled by a beautifully decked-out Battle of Britain class 4-6-2 Pacific?

This setting was adjacent to the Southern Region shed at Stewarts Lane. Golden Arrow motive power was always beautifully turned out here and the shed enjoyed the distinction of preparing locomotives for Royal Train duties.

THE DOWN 'GOLDEN ARROW' AT BATTERSEA

CITY OF WELLS AT STEWART'S LANE

Preserved Railways

I have visited many heritage railways over the years, as sketchbooks bursting with scrawled notes and scribbles will testify. These have proved to be invaluable sources of ideas and reference in the creation of new paintings. Also, the joys of these visits were the opportunities they presented to meet and talk to ex-railway personnel. There is always an element of good humour, banter and anecdote attached to these occasions.

Hearing about some of the things they used to get up to during those smokey, smelly, dirty, oily, greasy wonderful days makes me wonder how the railways ran efficiently or, indeed, if they ever did!

How do you spot a trainspotter?

Capturing live images of steam is not always as easy as it seems. Finding the right angle and composition is the first target. Completing in whatever time is available is another. Can you believe that a train will steam away whilst you are in the middle of your creative flight just to keep to a timetable. Rather thoughtless don't you think?!!!

Seriously though, the dedicated artist should be primed with an ability to capture enough of a subject in the time and circumstances available. There are occasions when time is not of the essence though.

I remember travelling to Dai Woodham's scrapyard at Barry Island in the early eighties to produce some oil sketches of the sad scene. Setting up the easel in the belief that I had all the time in the world to produce some hopefully moving works, I was in for a rude awakening. The local kids had taken over the place as an adventure playground. I was made immediately aware of this by the odd pebble or two bouncing off the canvas and... the back of my head! Despite this I was able to produce about seventeen oil sketches over a long weekend.

Time passed quickly, and I vowed to return at a later date under the misguided assumption that the hundreds of rusty, sad and forgotten locos would still be there for some time to come. How wrong can you be? We are all aware of the astonishing restoration miracle that occurred. I am just grateful that I was able to witness the amazing the scene and capture it on canvas for posterity.

RAIL, RUST & DANDELIONS

The interchange of locomotives at any given preserved railway is a great boon to the transport artist. Say the period picture you are working on is a Southern Region scene in the later fifties and includes an unrebuilt Battle of Britain class Bulleid Pacific.

What a joy to find a fully restored example turn up as a guest loco at your favourite railway. Accurate in every detail, it beats every bit of old black and white archive material. Even if it is a bit too shiny and polished for the occasion, it doesn't stretch the artist's imagination too much to 'scruffy' it up a little and simulate the working conditions of the time.

These sketches/scribbles were produced at various preserved railways. Their Spring Galas however, can sometimes be very wet and cold occasions.
A 4B pencil in frozen, shivering and shaking hands is not the most ideal way of gathering reference material.

Then, the prospect of thawing out in front of a roaring log fire whilst quaffing an ale or two at a local village watering hole does hold a certain appeal.

Two WSR.
fitters

THE NEW RAILWAY CHILDREN

WILLITON WAITING

PRESERVATION PERFECTION

The End

or is it just the beginning?

The Alan Ward Railway Sketchbook
www.alanwardcollection.co.uk

Published by Mainline & Maritime Ltd
3 Broadleaze, Upper Seagry, Nr Chippenham SN15 5EY
www.mainlineandmaritime.co.uk